D0056402

BRITAIN IN PICTURES

THE BRITISH PEOPLE IN PICTURES

BRITISH JOURNALISTS AND NEWSPAPERS

GENERAL EDITOR
W. J. TURNER

BRITISH JOURNALISTS AND NEWSPAPERS

DEREK HUDSON

WITH
8 PLATES IN COLOUR
AND
26 ILLUSTRATIONS IN
BLACK & WHITE

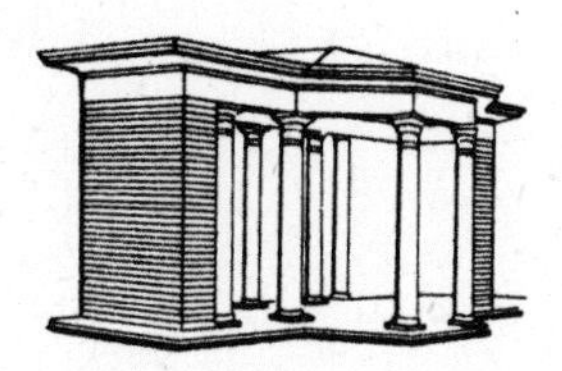

COLLINS · 14 ST. JAMES'S PLACE · LONDON
MCMXXXXV

PRODUCED BY
ADPRINT LIMITED LONDON

PRINTED IN GREAT BRITAIN BY
CLARKE & SHERWELL LTD NORTHAMPTON
ON MELLOTEX BOOK PAPER MADE BY
TULLIS RUSSELL & CO LTD MARKINCH SCOTLAND

LIST OF ILLUSTRATIONS

PLATES IN COLOUR

TEMPLE BAR AND ST. DUNSTAN'S CHURCH
Oil painting c. 1750

JOHN BELL 1745-1831
Coloured cartoon by Richard Dighton, 1824

THOMAS BARNES 1785-1841
Miniature by Sir William Newton, 1832

CARICATURES OF LONDON PAPERS
Coloured cartoon from *Maclean's Monthly Sheet of Caricatures*, 1833

GEORGE AUGUSTUS SALA 1828-1896
Coloured cartoon by Ape from *Vanity Fair*, September, 1875

ALFRED HARMSWORTH 1865-1922
Coloured cartoon by Spy, 1895

J. L. GARVIN
Coloured cartoon by Sir Max Beerbohm

A FORECAST OF LONDON'S AIR-RAID DEFENCE AS SHOWN AT THE WEMBLEY PARK EXHIBITION IN 1924
Coloured reproduction in *The Illustrated London News* from a drawing by Steven Spurrier

BLACK AND WHITE ILLUSTRATIONS

PAGE

THE FAITHFUL POST, JULY, 1653 — 5
Initial
By courtesy of the London Press Club

MERCURIUS AULICUS, NO. 1, JANUARY, 1643 — 7
Detail from the heading
By courtesy of the London Press Club

FRONT PAGE OF *MERCURIUS CIVICUS*, FEBRUARY, 1643 — 9
By courtesy of the Curators of the Bodleian Library, Oxford

FRONT PAGE OF *A PERFECT DIURNALL OF THE PASSAGES IN PARLIAMENT*, FEBRUARY, 1642 — 11
By courtesy of the Curators of the Bodleian Library, Oxford

THE SCOTTISH DOVE, JANUARY, 1643 — 12
"An Antidote against the poisoned insinuations of the *Mercurius Aulicus*"
By courtesy of the London Press Club

THE POST BOY, OCTOBER, 1709 — 13
Detail from the heading
By courtesy of the London Press Club

SIR ROGER L'ESTRANGE, 1616-1704 — 15
Engraving by R. White after an oil painting by Kneller
By courtesy of the London Press Club

THE MAIDSTONE MERCURY, 1725 — 16
Detail from the heading
By courtesy of the London Press Club

SIR RICHARD STEELE, 1672-1729 — 18
Engraving by Houbraken after Kneller
By courtesy of the National Museum of Wales, Cardiff

DANIEL DEFOE, c. 1659-1731 — 19
Engraving by Van der Gucht from *British Portrait Engravings*

THE GENTLEMAN'S MAGAZINE, Vol. 1, 1731 — 21
Detail from the front page

JOHN WILKES, 1727-1797 — 23
Engraving dated 1786 from Wilkes's autographed copy of Homer's *Ilias* (Greek & Latin, Cambridge, 1686)
By courtesy of the Trustees of the British Museum

WILLIAM WOODFALL, OR 'MEMORY' WOODFALL, 1746-1803 — 26
Engraving in the possession of the Newspaper Press Fund

PAGE

JAMES PERRY, 1756-1821 — 27
Cartoon by Richard Dighton, published in the *Morning Chronicle*, 1824
By courtesy of the London Press Club

THE TIMES OR *DAILY UNIVERSAL REGISTER*, January 1st, 1788 — 28
Detail from the heading of the 1st number
By courtesy of the Proprietors of The Times

THE TIMES PRINTING PRESS INVENTED AND CONSTRUCTED BY APPLEGATH AND COWPER, *THE TIMES* ENGINEERS, 1827 — 29
By courtesy of the Proprietors of The Times

JOHN WALTER II, 1776-1847 — 31
Miniature by an unknown artist
By courtesy of John Walter, Esq.

LEIGH HUNT, 1784-1859 — 32
Engraving by A. Crowquill

JOHN THADEUS DELANE, 1817-1879 — 34
Photograph by Ernest Edwards
By courtesy of the Proprietors of The Times

SIR WILLIAM HOWARD RUSSELL, 1820-1907 — 35
Cartoon by Ape from *Vanity Fair*, 1875
By courtesy of the London Press Club

THE FIRE OF HAMBURG — 37
Engraving from *The Illustrated London News*, 1st number, May 1842
By courtesy of The Illustrated London News

T. P. O'CONNOR, 1848-1929 — 39
Cartoon by Spy from *Vanity Fair*, 1888
By courtesy of the London Press Club

THE LONDON PRESS — 40
Details from a Humorous Survey of Periodical Titles printed on a handkerchief
Early nineteenth century
By courtesy of the London Press Club

LORD BEAVERBROOK — 43
Cartoon by David Low
By courtesy of the Artist and the Evening Standard

C. P. SCOTT, 1846-1931 — 44
Bronze by Jacob Epstein
By courtesy of the Artist and the Manchester City Art Gallery

LUDGATE BRIDGE AND ST. PAUL'S AS SEEN FROM FLEET STREET — 47
Etching by Dorothy Sweet
By courtesy of R. F. Sampson & Co. Ltd.

I

THE Press is one of the most important institutions in Britain, but it is surprising how little is generally known of its history. According to a survey prepared by the London Press Exchange, the circulation of morning papers in 1934 was about ninety-five for every hundred families, and each family took in an average of 1 3/10ths newspapers on Sundays; yet how many of these readers, one wonders, could give even a single significant name or date in the story of the long struggle for liberty of the Press.

Despite the frequent revelations and confessions of journalists, the modern newspaper's methods of working also remain mysterious to most people. The makers of a newspaper are "they" ; the paper is "it." Their readers realise that the papers emanate, to a large extent, from the Fleet Street neighbourhood of London, and in passing they look with a vague awe at their dingy or chromium-plated offices; but such is the power and authority of the printed word that they are reluctant positively to identify the groundlings whom they see passing in and out of these office doorways as the upholders of the dignity of "the fourth Estate."

The reluctance may be understandable, for journalists in their working clothes are not invariably impressive; but the respectful interest remains. The public attitude towards journalists in the eighteenth century and to-day differs as widely as the popular opinion of a snake and a fox terrier. In the course of this book we shall consider some of the men who were responsible for bringing about this change from distrust to confidence—from Dr. Johnson's verdict that journalists were "without a Wish for Truth, or Thought of Decency" to Mr. Churchill's declaration in 1943 that "our vast influential newspaper press has known how to combine independence and liveliness with discretion and patriotism."

For well over a hundred years Fleet Street has beckoned and inspired some of the best of our young men. It might have been yesterday that David Copperfield "tamed that savage stenographic mystery" and "joined with eleven others in reporting the debates in Parliament for a Morning Newspaper," wallowing in words; or his contemporary young Pendennis arrived at a newspaper office "with his manuscripts in his pocket, and with a great deal of bustle and pleasure such as a man feels at the outset of his literary career, when to see himself in print is still a novel sensation, and he yet pleases himself that his writings are creating some noise in the world." The Copperfields and Pendennises may from time to time go off to the wars; but they come back again. Fresh currents and impetuous tributaries will always keep the stream of Fleet Street life alive.

II

A book about journalists might conceivably begin with the days when men lived "cavily in a cave" and Taffy of the *Just So Stories* drew informative pictures on bits of bark. But we shall come more directly to our subject by taking down the appropriate volume of the Oxford English Dictionary and extracting from it the definition that the journalist is one "who earns his living by editing or writing for a public journal or journals." To which may usefully be added Mr. Stanley Morison's opinion, that "yearly, quarterly or monthly measures of frequency may constitute the Periodical, but publication more often than once a month is essential to a Journal."

News letters, written by friends or agents to merchants and statesmen, preceded and were for a long time co-existent with printed news. Already in the sixteenth century occasional news ballads and pamphlets were being printed, often in defiance of the law. Typical of these was a pamphlet of news about the Council of Trent published in 1549. They were isolated productions, in which the news by modern standards was usually stale, and in which there was no continuity of publication. The earliest attempt at regular journalism was probably the "Weekly Newes from Italy, Germanie, Hungaria," first published by Nicholas Bourne and Thomas Archer on May 23, 1622. The public approved this idea of a continuous series; the news-book became known as a "courant," or, more often, a "coranto"; and almost from the first it bore a serial number. The author of one of these corantos wrote in a strain not unworthy of the Foreign Department of *The Times*:

> "I can assure you, there is not a line printed nor proposed to your view, but carries the credit of other Originalls, and justifies itself from honest and understanding authority; so that if they should faile there in true and exact discoveries, be not you too malignant against the Printer here, that is so far from any invention of his owne, that when he meets with improbability or absurdity, hee leaves it quite out rather than he will startle your patience . . ."

Despite their serial numbers, these early news-books were by no means consistent in their titles, and were often headed simply "The Continuation

(413)

Letters intercepted from the King, Queene, L. Digby, and Iermin, to the Lord Goring in France.
Bandon-bridge neere Chester taken by Sir Thomas Fairfax.
The Irish Rebels joyned with Cardinall Williams in Wales.

Numb. 40

Mercurius Civicus.

LONDONS INTELLIGENCER:

OR,

Truth impartially related from thence to the whole Kingdome, to prevent mis-information.

From *Thursday February* 22. to *Thursday February*. 29. 1643.

THe interest which every good subject hath in the actions of the King and Parliament, is sufficient to defend him from the imputation of being a Busiebodie, in maintaining the Justice of them; That, and my desire not onely to give satisfaction unto my countreymen in the most certaine intelligence that should come to my hands, but also to admonish (especially the

Rr City

Front Page of *Mercurius Civicus: London's Intelligencer*, February, 1643 of our Former Newes," or "More Newes for this Present Week." Their lives were short, and in the later years of James I's reign they succeeded one another with bewildering rapidity. The names of Nicholas Bourne and Thomas Archer appeared on the title-pages of several of them; but it was Nathaniel Butter who was the moving spirit—both as writer, printer and publisher—in this earliest epoch of English journalism; and it is Butter who is caricatured as Cymbal, the manager of "The Staple of News," in Ben Jonson's play of that name.

Thanks to the stern censorship of Star Chamber, the *corantos* were permitted to deal only with foreign news. In 1632 even this privilege was taken away from them, on the complaint of the Spanish Ambassador, and for six years there were no pamphlets—until in 1638 Charles I granted a monopoly for printing foreign news to Butter and Bourne. Despite his energy and success, Butter cannot have made journalism profitable; Smith's "Obituary" recorded his death in 1664 as "Nath. Butter, an old stationer, died very poor."

The abolition of Star Chamber in February, 1641, paved the way for the first English periodical of domestic news, the *Diurnall Occurrences in Parliament*, published the following November. The word "Diurnall" meant not a daily publication but a day by day record for publication once a week. Many other Diurnalls appeared in 1641-2, notably Samuel Pecke's *A Perfect Diurnall* with its entertaining picture on the title page of the House of Commons in session; and then for a time the word *Passages* distinguished the accounts of parliamentary proceedings. The Civil War brought a remarkable advance; for not only did it provide important news that everyone was anxious to hear, but both sides had an interest in exploiting it. Corantos and Diurnalls gave place to the most famous of all the early news-books, the Mercuries.

The first of our English Mercuries, written in the Royalist cause, was begun in January, 1643, at Oxford, where Charles I had established his court after Edgehill. It was called *Mercurius Aulicus* and appeared every Sunday for about three years. *Mercurius Aulicus* at once proved a serious challenge to the parliamentary Diurnalls, which hitherto had had things all their own way; and it was actually sold in London by the hawkers and "mercury women"—not without grave risk to themselves.

Sir John Berkenhead, of Oriel College, was the author-in-chief of *Aulicus*. He was assisted by Dr. Peter Heylin and others, and his journal easily surpassed the Diurnalls in literary merit. Aubrey showed a marked dislike for Berkenhead personally, and though conceding that he was "exceedingly confident" and "witty," maintained that he had "great goggli eies" and "would lye damnably." The formal reply to Berkenhead was at first undertaken without notable success by Captain Thomas Audley, "a swarthy chest-nut coloured captaine" who lived in Bloomsbury, "near the great cherry garden," a neighbourhood that has since been the haunt of

(1) Numb. 38

A PERFECT DIVRNALL OF THE PASSAGES In Parliament:

From the 27. of Febr. to the 6. of March.

Collected by the same hand that formerly drew up the Copy for William Cook *of Furnifalls Inne, and now printed by* J. Okes, Fr. Leach, *and are to be sold by* Fr. Coles *in the Old Baily.* 1642.

The relation of the oath of the Lord Bro

Munday the 27. of February.

THe House of Commons this day proceeded in their debate for the speedy expediating of their votes for a Treaty and Cessation of Armes, and the Propositions from the Lord Generall for the limitation and qualification of the said Cessation, and fully agreeing upon the same they added two further votes concerning the said businesse, very necessary and fitting to be condiscended unto, to this effect, viz. That the said Treaty and Cessation of Armes shall bee no hinderance to any proceedings concerning the association of the Counties, or the leavying of monies upon the Propositions, or weekely contributions for the maintenance of the Army, and they also voted that they would not accept of a Treaty with any persons to be appointed by his Majesty, without his Majesty himselfe in Parliament.

Pp Which

FRONT PAGE OF

A PERFECT DIURNALL OF THE PASSAGES IN PARLIAMENT, FEBRUARY, 1642

(97) Numb.13.

holy innocency is blessed

Be Wise as Serpents, Innocent as Doves.

THE

SCOTISH DOVE,

Sent out, and Returning;

Bringing Intelligence from the Armies, and makes some Relations of other observable Passages of both Kingdoms, for Information and Instruction.

As an Antidote against the poisoned insinuations of Mercurius Aulicus, *and the errours of other intelligencers.*

THE SCOTTISH DOVE, JANUARY, 1643

other weekly journalists; but his paper, *Mercurius Britanicus*, showed vast improvement after he had handed it over, in 1644, to a prolific, ingenious rogue, with "trapstick" legs and a large stomach, called Marchamont Nedham.

They did not provide a very hopeful augury for the future of journalism —these time-serving hack-writers of the Civil War. Nedham was no more reputable than the others, but for several years he showed himself the equal of Berkenhead. Eventually he changed sides and conducted *Mercurius Pragmaticus* for the King. The Mercuries themselves, though hastily printed and unimpressive to look at, had certain features in common with twentieth century newspapers. One of these was a running summary of their contents, printed as an "ear" on the first page. Thus Number 8, dated July 13, 1643, of the royalist *Mercurius Civicus, Londons Intelligencer*, had the following "ear": "The King and Queen conjoyn'd, The Kentish news related, Our Forces are united, A publique Fast appointed." The same paper regularly printed portraits of Charles and Henrietta Maria, and on one occasion a portrait of Prince Rupert, so that it may be considered the earliest forerunner of such a journal as the *Illustrated London News*.

That the news-writers of the Civil War should have abused the relative freedom afforded them by the suppression of Star Chamber is not surprising, and there was some justification for the system of licensing imposed by the Long Parliament in 1643, against which Milton thundered in his *Areopagitica*. But the ordinance seems to have had no effect on the spate of royalist Mercuries which were soon being printed in London itself, and which even continued to appear in London after its occupation by the Army in December, 1648. Under such servants of the Parliament as Samuel Pecke and Henry Walker, various *Intelligencers*, *Posts*, *Spies* and *Scouts* appeared on that side; and, after the death of Charles I, we find the astonishing Marchamont Nedham turning his coat once again and becoming for ten years the official journalist of the Commonwealth.

Mercurius Politicus—notable for its leading article—was now the vehicle for Nedham's flippancies, and it was at its best in 1651 and 1652, when John Milton, then censor of the press, succeeded in influencing its contents. After the break-up of the Commonwealth, however, even the ever-obliging Nedham could no longer hold his job. General Monck's Council of State authorised the following announcement in March, 1660:

> "Whereas *Marchemont Nedham*, the Author of the Weekly News books, called *Mercurius Politicus*, and the *Publique Intelligencer*, is, by Order of the Council of the State, discharged from Writing or Publishing any Publique Intelligence: The Reader is desired to take notice, that by Order of the said Council, *Henry Muddiman* and *Giles Dury*, are authorised henceforth to Write and Publish the said *Intelligence* . . ."

The appearance on the scene of Henry Muddiman began a new phase in the history of journalism—a phase that was to see the publication of the first newspaper properly so called. Of the early pioneers—from Nathaniel Butter to Berkenhead and Nedham—whose work we have so rapidly surveyed, the best that can be said is that, though weak in honesty, they had qualities of patience, perseverance, and abundant self-confidence.

THE POST BOY

III

When he superseded Nedham, Henry Muddiman was thirty years old and a London schoolmaster. Pepys called him a "good scholar." For a short period after the restoration the Press was relatively free, and Muddiman would have been in a better position than any previous journalist if the House of Commons had not passed a resolution in June, 1660, forbidding the printing of reports of its proceedings without special permission. This was a great blow to him, and the sale of his news-books soon declined; but the prohibition favoured the circulation of written news-letters, which for this reason continued to exist and to compete with printed news. As Muddiman had a privilege of free postage, he was able to carry on an exceedingly profitable business in these written news-letters, and for a time possessed a practical monopoly of the output of news.

From Nathaniel Butter's day, the nave of St. Paul's had been used as a promenade for news-mongers—and this was one reason why so many printing offices were established in the neighbourhood of Fleet Street. Those who were responsible for written news-letters would return from St. Paul's or some other meeting-place to dictate their "copy" to groups of scriveners, who transcribed the news on three sides of a folded sheet, leaving wide margins for the insertion of "stop-press" matter. The letters would then be folded and addressed on the fourth side to the merchant or diplomat, county squire or coffee house proprietor, who had subscribed for them. Muddiman's charge for news-letters was £5 a year.

It was not long before Muddiman was challenged in his authority by Roger L'Estrange, a Royalist pamphleteer with a powerful pen, who certainly deserved some reward for his services. In 1662 L'Estrange was granted a general warrant for the seizure of seditious books and their writers. He has often been criticised for his stern treatment of a printer called John Twyn; but there is evidence that Twyn was not undeserving of punishment. After the passing of the Licensing Act, L'Estrange's influence increased, and in 1663 he was appointed Surveyor of the Press, *i.e.*, censor of all printed matter, with the sole right of publishing news-books hitherto enjoyed by Muddiman. In this capacity he organised the pamphlets known as the *Intelligencer* and the *Newes*. But L'Estrange proved as unpopular a newsmonger as Muddiman was popular; and his enemy Joseph Williamson, Under Secretary of State, seized the opportunity of employing Muddiman against him in an enterprise which resulted in the publication of our first genuine newspaper.

In 1665 the Court was at Oxford, owing to the plague, and it was at Oxford that there appeared on November 16 of that year the first number of the bi-weekly *Oxford Gazette*, organised by Williamson and written by Muddiman. As J. B. Williams remarks, "Any question of infringement of L'Estrange's patent would have been difficult to raise at Oxford, within

SIR ROGER L'ESTRANGE, 1616-1704
Engraving by R. White after an oil painting by Kneller

the privileges of the University." And Charles and his courtiers were glad to have the new paper, for the possibility of infection kept their hands off L'Estrange's London news-books.

The *Oxford Gazette* consisted of "half a sheet in folio," 2 inches by 6½, closely printed in two columns on both sides—exactly the same size as Muddiman's news-letters, to which it was obviously intended as a supplement, and easily folded up with them. This makes it clear that our newspapers developed directly from the written news-letters, not from the printed pamphlets (and incidentally reminds us that the publication of news-letters by Commander Stephen King-Hall and others in the reign of King George VI was no innovation, but a reversion to an old principle). Pepys thought the paper "very pretty, full of newes and no folly in it." Leader-writers may well ponder this judgment, for by "no folly" Pepys meant that there was no leading article.

With its twenty-fourth number, *The Oxford Gazette* became *The London Gazette*, and it has been published under this title ever since. L'Estrange soon gave up the attempt to rival it with another paper, the *Publick Intelligence*; but on appealing to the King he received a handsome subsidy for his news-books and was confirmed in his office as Surveyor of the Press. He took a leading part in bringing Titus Oates to justice, and in 1681 began *The Observator*, keeping up a vigorous argument with Oates's journalists in the form of a debate between a "typical" Tory—who of course had the best of it—and a "typical" Whig. Hard things have been said of L'Estrange, "the first Tory." Macaulay wrote of his "mean and flippant jargon" and his "ferocious and ignoble nature." But this cultivated translator of Aesop and Erasmus wrote excellent English and is not a little to be admired for the way in which as "a gentleman and an old fellow of sixty-eight"—to use his own words—he "descended into the kennel to lash a pack of curs."

On the whole the later years of Charles II's reign and the three years in which James II was on the throne were not propitious for journalists. But on the very day of James's flight, December 12, 1688, three new papers were started. In 1695 the Licensing Act was not renewed, and soon the restrictions on the periodical press, which had been in force for so long, were raised. The immediate result of this, and of the establishment of postal services, was a swarm of *Postmen* and *Post-boys*—as many as twenty-one papers, according to Fox Bourne, being published in each week, besides *The London Gazette*. Yet still the news-letters held their own, with the difference that many of them were now printed. Between 1696 and 1716, Ichabod Dawks's news-letters flourished, printed in a beautiful script type. Dawks had a delightful name, a fine type, and withal a kindly heart. This is how he concluded his news-letter for the last day of 1698:

> "The Old Year being ended, I wish all my Worthy Customers, Friends and the Nation in general a Happy New Year, that we may all Live in the Fear and Service of God, in Dutiful Subjection to His Majesty, in Brotherly Love and Charity one towards another, that when this Life is ended we may all enjoy a Blessed Eternity, to which I heartily say, Amen."

THE MAIDSTONE MERCURY

TEMPLE BAR AND ST. DUNSTAN'S CHURCH

Oil painting c. 1750

By courtesy of the London Press Club

JOHN BELL, 1745-1831
Coloured cartoon by Richard Dighton, 1824
By courtesy of the London Press Club

IV

The reign of Anne was of the utmost importance to journalism. Not only did it contain such landmarks as the passing of a law giving copyright to authors, and the imposition of a stamp tax and duty on advertisements, but it saw the appearance on March 2, 1702—three days after the Queen had ascended the throne—of the first English daily paper, *The Daily Courant*.

Our first daily published nothing but news, "supposing other people to have sense enough to make reflections for themselves." The first nine issues were printed on one side alone, but *The Daily Courant* progressed steadily and expanded to four pages, and even for a time to six. The paper seems also to have had more than a single edition, for corrections were made in the course of a day's issue. A note to No. 1838 reads: "In some of yesterday's *Courants*, the nineteenth line of the second column of the first page, for *favour* read *friendship*."

This sturdy pioneer was continued until 1735. The first paper to use the word "evening" in its title, *The Evening Post*, appeared in 1706; but it was only one of a number of publications to come out in the evenings three times a week.

The history of the Press in Scotland followed roughly the same course as it had done in England, though at a distance. Scotland had its *Mercurius Caledonius* (1661) edited by Thomas Sydserf, the first Scottish journalist, but the earliest Scottish periodical that may properly be called a newspaper, *The Edinburgh Gazette*, did not appear until 1699, to be followed by *The Edinburgh Evening Courant* in 1705. *The Dublin Gazette* was also started in the latter year. Scotland's chief contribution to the early history of journalism lay in the fact that Daniel Defoe edited his *Review* from Edinburgh intermittently between 1707 and 1711.

In Defoe arose a journalist very different from the conscientious Muddiman, the arch-Tory L'Estrange (really an astrigent forerunner of Colonel Blimp), or the homely Ichabod Dawks. Defoe had engaged strenuously in pamphleteering for many years before 1702, when he wrote his *Shortest Way with the Dissenters* and found a reward offered for his arrest. He was then, according to the advertisement, "a middle-sized spare man, about forty years old, of a brown complexion, and dark brown-coloured hair, but wears a wig; a hooked nose, a sharp chin, grey eyes, and a large mole near his mouth." Pilloried in July, 1703, Defoe composed a "Hymn to the Pillory" which sold well among the friendly crowd and contained the famous lines:

> "Tell them the men that placed him here
> Are scandals to the times;
> Are at a loss to find his guilt
> And can't commit his crimes."

SIR RICHARD STEELE, 1672-1729
Engraving by Houbraken after Kneller

While imprisoned in Newgate he began his *Weekly Review of the Affairs of France*, soon altered to *A Review of the State of the English Nation*, which he continued to write, from different parts of Britain, until 1713.

The *Review* is best considered as a landmark in the history of journalism, rather than an item in the history of newspapers. It was not really a newspaper; but it contained better writing and far more interesting and constructive criticism than anything that had preceded it. Unfortunately Defoe had to vary his principles in order to keep his journal, and himself, alive; nevertheless, the *Review* helped to create a new class of reader of which in due course the newspapers had to take note. One of the first to compete with Defoe in this new journalism was Richard Steele who, on April 12, 1709, began *The Tatler*.

Steele was the son of an Irish attorney and had been born in Dublin in 1672. Gay, impetuous, charming, and at the same time sincere, he was an essayist who would have had little to learn of the many successors, from Lamb to Lucas, who have followed the line of periodical literature he initiated. Not the least significant of his characteristics was his happiness in marriage; and to his essay on that subject, at once graceful and profound, new readers of Steele may confidently be directed.

It has often been said, nevertheless, that Steele is chiefly to be remembered for having obtained the collaboration of Joseph Addison in *The Tatler*, and in its more ambitious successor, *The Spectator*, which followed it on March 1, 1711. This is a misrepresentation. What is true is that much of the success of both these papers, and of their sequel *The Guardian*, was due to the stimulus of friendly rivalry provided by the

DANIEL DEFOE c. 1659-1731
Engraving by Van der Gucht

association of the two friends. Here was the golden age, all too brief, of eighteenth century journalism. Steele's famous trilogy is not the sum of it; for he and Addison, as Whigs, were outmatched in political argument by Jonathan Swift in the Tory *Examiner*—and the *Examiner*, started in 1710, was a newspaper; Steele's papers and Defoe's *Review* were not.

Yet Swift was no less scurrilous than his contemporaries, and it was owing to Steele and Addison that the Press was for a few years in a comparatively healthy condition. A list of 1709 gives no fewer than eighteen publications that were then being published each week.

The Stamp Act, imposing a tax of a halfpenny on papers of half a sheet and a penny on papers of a whole sheet, came into force on August 1, 1712. It had a profound influence on journalism, but did not in the long run produce the crippling results which Swift feared when he wrote: "The *Observator* is fallen; the *Medleys* are jumbled together in the *Flying Post*; the *Examiner* is deadly sick; the *Spectator* keeps up and doubles its price." Paradoxically the levying of the duty resulted in an increase in the size of the journals, and Mr. Stanley Morison has conjectured that this was due to a loophole in the drafting of the Act, by which papers of six pages succeeded in evading the tax. The distinction between the news journals and the purely literary papers, such as Steele founded, henceforth tended to disappear; for in order to fill his enlarged paper the editor of a news journal was compelled to include essay material and the literary paper to give news and politics. This was the beginning of weekly papers as we now know them.

V

The newspapers survived the Stamp Act, and indeed increased in number; but they gradually lost their newly-won integrity. Steele remained honest, but after 1712 politics became his main interest. He began to speak out loud and bold, and in 1714, despite eloquent speeches in his defence, was expelled from the House of Commons on account of certain articles in *The Englishman* and *The Crisis*. The episode showed that, while the Crown no longer controlled the Press, the Ministers of the Crown were able to take their revenge on individuals. As Sir Robert Walpole put it in his defence of Steele: "The liberty of the press is unrestrained; how then shall a part of the legislature dare to punish that as a crime which is not declared to be so by any law passed by the whole?"

Both the answer to this question and the reason for the general deterioration in the quality of journalism lay in the increasing bitterness of party politics. It is impossible, in this compressed essay, to enter into the details of the warfare of words in the early years of George I's reign. Defoe was still brilliantly at work, now in Mist's *Journal* or in Applebee's, and he had a hand in 1719 in starting our second daily paper *The Daily Post*; the Whigs also possessed able writers in John Trenchard and Thomas Gordon of *The London Journal*; but the next new publication to make a definite impression was *The Craftsman*, edited by Nicholas Amhurst, which appeared in 1726 and incidentally set the fashion for an exaggerated use of italic in the text.

William Pulteney wrote for *The Craftsman*, and to it Bolingbroke contributed his scathing "Remarks on the History of England" under the pseudonym of "Humphrey Oldcastle"—letters deserving to rank in eighteenth century satire alongside those of Swift and Junius.

The name of Nicholas Amhurst prompts a digression, for it suggests a by-way in English journalism which has been insufficiently explored. Amhurst's *Terrae Filius*, a satire on Oxford published in 1721, is generally looked upon as the first university periodical—forerunner of Thomas Warton's *The Student* (1750); of William Morris's *Oxford and Cambridge Magazine* (1856), to which Rossetti and Burne Jones contributed; and of so many other Oxford journals, which have published the early work of such writers as Swinburne, Lewis Carroll, Quiller-Couch, Oscar Wilde, Max Beerbohm and Hilaire Belloc. The story of university journalism at Cambridge is equally interesting. Mr. H. C. Marillier's privately printed monograph on "University Magazines" and a short article in the Cambridge History of English Literature are apparently the only serious studies that have so far been made of a subject which would amply repay further attention.

We have seen that reports of parliamentary debates had been forbidden since the Restoration. Partially successful attempts had been made to

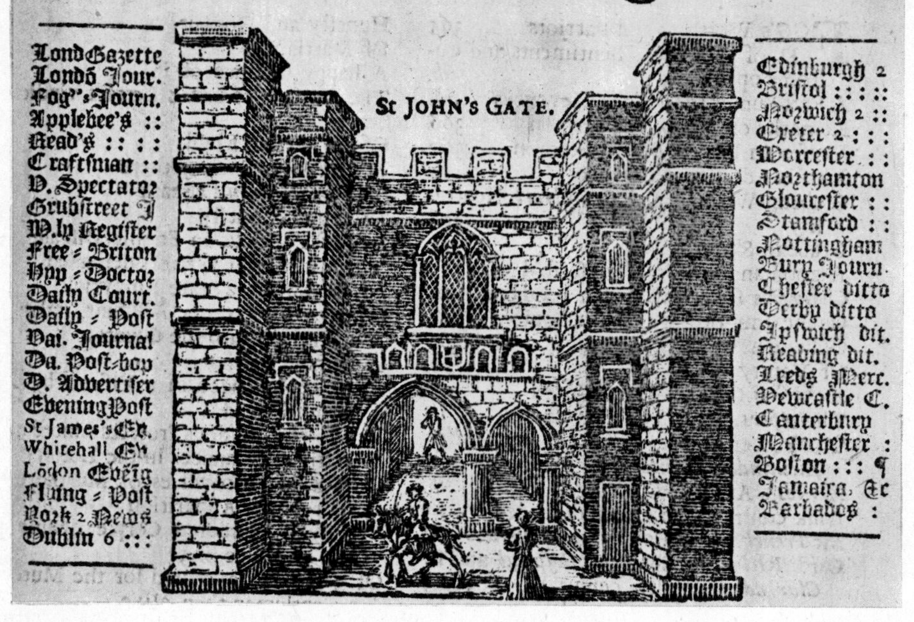
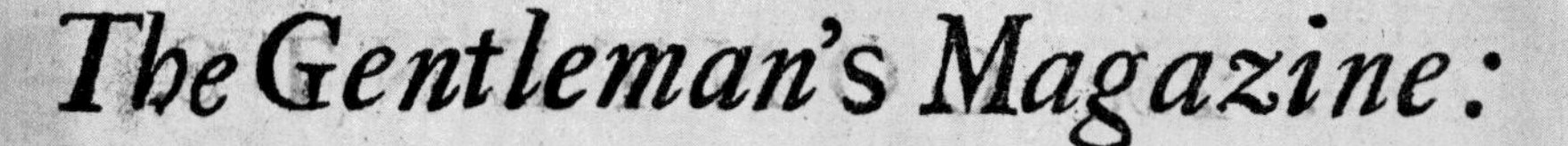

The Gentleman's Magazine:

ST JOHN'S GATE.

Lond Gazette
Londõ Jour.
Fog's Journ.
Applebee's ::
Read's ::::
Craftsman ::
D. Spectator
Grubstreet J
W.ly Register
Free = Briton
Hyp = Doctor
Daily Court.
Daily = Post
Dai. Journal
Da. Post-boy
D. Advertiser
Evening Post
St James's Ev.
Whitehall Ev.
Lõdon Evẽig
Flying = Post
York 2 News
Dublin 6 :::

Edinburgh 2
Bristol ::::
Norwich 2 ::
Exeter 2 :::
Worcester ::
Northamton
Gloucester ::
Stamford ::
Nottingham
Bury Journ.
Chester ditto
Derby ditto
Ipswich dit.
Reading dit.
Leeds Merc.
Newcastle C.
Canterbury
Manchester :
Boston ::: ¶
Jamaica, &c
Barbados :

THE GENTLEMAN'S MAGAZINE, Vol. 1, 1731
Detail from the front page

circumvent this prohibition, but the House of Commons still regarded it seriously and in 1722 resolved that "no newswriters do presume . . . to intermeddle with the debates." Nevertheless, Edward Cave, who began *The Gentleman's Magazine* in 1731, under the famous pseudonym "Sylvanus Urban," published lengthy reports of Parliament from 1736 onwards, to begin with giving only the first and last letters of the speakers' names, and later pretending that they were accounts of the "debates in the senate of Great Lilliput." Dr. Johnson wrote a good deal for the *Gentleman's*; and between 1740 and 1743 he was responsible to Cave for the parliamentary reports. Sir John Hawkins tells us that years afterwards, when Johnson and some friends were discussing a speech by Pitt, Johnson declared "That speech I wrote in a garret in Exeter Street," and he went on to explain:

> "I never was in the House of Commons but once. Cave had interest with the doorkeeper. He and the persons under him got admittance. They brought away the subject of discussion, the names of the speakers, the side they took, and the

order in which they rose, together with notes of the various arguments . . . The whole was afterwards communicated to me, and I composed the speeches in the form they have now in 'Parliamentary Debates'."

Boswell admits that shortly before his death Johnson "expressed his regret for his having been the author of fictions which had passed for realities." Yet various letters of Cave's quoted by Boswell show that at times Cave went to much trouble to obtain a reliable precis of the speeches. *The Gentleman's Magazine* continued for the better part of two centuries. It was the first journal to use the title "magazine," and a set of its yearly volumes is now a treasure in any library. Praed, writing a hundred years after its foundation, told us of a Vicar who

> "Wrote, too, in a quiet way,
> Small treatises, and smaller verses,
> And sage remarks on chalk and clay,
> And hints to noble Lords—and nurses;
> True histories of last year's ghost,
> Lines to a ringlet, or a turban,
> And trifles for the Morning Post,
> And nothings for Sylvanus Urban."

"Nothings" they may have seemed to contemporaries, but those curious bits and pieces of information have proved their worth to posterity. *The Gentleman's Magazine* has its place in journalistic history and its founder Edward Cave—a reserved and gouty gentleman of sedentary habits, who drank milk and water and played shuttlecock—deserves a salute from all historians.

The *Gentleman's* was not the only production to show that eighteenth century journalism, though in general deserving the strictures that Dr Johnson lavished on it, could rise occasionally above the level of "Grub Street."

In 1745 the robust voice of Henry Fielding—who had already edited *The Champion*, an imitation of the *Spectator*, and the forerunner of John Scott's Sunday paper of the same name—began to be heard in *The True Patriot*. "I do not live within a mile of Grub Street," declared the author of *Tom Jones*, "nor am I acquainted with a single inhabitant of that place. I am of no party—a word which I hope, by these my labours, to eradicate out of our constitution . . ."

But *The True Patriot* was, in fact, a government organ, which lasted no longer than the Pretender whom it was designed to ridicule; and, despite various other attempts, the founder of the English novel left no real mark on English journalism.

John Wilkes, 1727-1797
Engraving dated 1786 from Wilkes's Autographed copy of Homer's *Ilias*

VI

By the end of George II's reign and the beginning of George III's, the newspapers were in a more flourishing condition—at least as regards size and circulation—than they had ever been. This was due partly to the general growth of British commerce and to the more settled state of the country after the 45; partly to the improvement in the posts; but chiefly to the emergence of advertising as a factor in newspaper finance which was to play a decisive part in securing freedom for the Press. This new importance of advertising is clearly indicated by the number of papers which from 1730, when *The Daily Advertiser* was founded, bore the name "advertiser" in their title. The discovery of advertising tended to take the newspapers out of the control of the printers and put them into the hands of groups of proprietors. *The Daily Advertiser*, by its combination of news and advertisements, has claims to be regarded as the first modern newspaper, and it maintained its separate existence until 1807.

Sensing a new stability in their affairs, the newspapers gradually came forward with more confidence as the champions of public opinion and the rights of the people against the Crown and its Ministers. From 1755 onwards *The Monitor* bravely attacked the corruption at court, and in 1762, after the unpopular Lord Bute had been made Prime Minister by George III, it came out with the reminder that "A wise prince ought to resolve never to give himself up totally to those he advances to power." The government case was entrusted to a new paper *The Briton*, under the editorship of Tobias Smollett—another successful novelist who was to prove less effective in journalism. The short-lived *Briton* is chiefly remembered because it gave rise to a pungent opponent in *The North Briton* of John Wilkes.

After Number 45 of *The North Briton* a "general warrant" was issued against its authors, printers and publishers. At his trial Wilkes was acquitted and general warrants were declared illegal—an extremely important reform. He was next accused of publishing an obscene libel, was outlawed, and for twenty years struggled (admittedly in a most provocative manner) to obtain his rights as a member of parliament.

It is paradoxical but undeniable that the career of this dissolute and unscrupulous adventurer led to a substantial enlargement of the liberty of the press, and greatly encouraged the advance of sound journalism. Courtesy and charm of manner, rather than any genuine democratic instinct, lay at the root of his success and of the remarkable popularity which sustained him in his reverses. Wilkes's secret is nowhere better revealed than in Boswell's description of how he conquered a hostile Dr Johnson by helping him to veal at a dinner party:

> " 'Pray give me leave, Sir;—It is better here—A little of the brown—Some fat, Sir—A little of the stuffing—Some gravy—Let me have the pleasure of giving you some butter—Allow me to recommend a squeeze of this orange; or the lemon, perhaps, may have more zest.'—'Sir, Sir, I am obliged to you, Sir,' cried Johnson, bowing, and turning his head to him with a look for some time of 'surly virtue,' but, in a short while, of complacency."

A far abler writer than Wilkes was the mysterious Junius, often identified as Sir Philip Francis, who contributed the first of his famous Letters to *The Public Advertiser* on April 28, 1767. In 1770 Henry Sampson Woodfall, the printer of this paper, was tried for publishing Junius's Letter to the King, and received what amounted to an acquittal. Soon afterwards John Almon and others organised some reports of Parliament in various papers. Reports were still technically forbidden, and these were couched in insulting terms. A proclamation of the House was issued against six

THOMAS BARNES, 1785-1841
Miniature by Sir William Newton, 1832
By courtesy of the Proprietors of The Times

CARICATURES OF LONDON PAPERS

Coloured cartoon from *The Looking Glass* or *Caricature Annual*, 1833

By courtesy of the Proprietors of The Times

printers, one of whom, Wheble of *The Middlesex Journal*—a paper founded to support John Wilkes—was arrested. By an ingenious stratagem he contrived his appearance at Guildhall on a day when Wilkes, newly appointed a magistrate, was sitting—and Wilkes promptly discharged him. The Lord Mayor and an alderman named Oliver supported Wilkes, and after complicated proceedings and vigorous attempts to assert its privileges—including the imprisonment of the Lord Mayor and Alderman Oliver (but not Wilkes)—Parliament yielded to the will of the people and admitted itself defeated. The debates have been reported ever since.

VII

In the wild and whirling days of the 1760's and 1770's, fresh newspapers were starting up and dying almost every month—and writers also had their brief careers and swift disappearances. One of these was Thomas Chatterton, who wrote for *The Middlesex Journal* and was praised by Wilkes, but who found that there was "no money to be got on this side of the question" and that even when his articles were accepted payment was often delayed. Before his eighteenth birthday he had put an end to his life.

Despite an increased stamp duty and a heavy tax on advertisements, the newspapers on the whole flourished, for the appetite of the public had been aroused. George Crabbe expressed his amazement at the number of papers on sale:

> "For, soon as morning dawns with roseate hue,
> The 'Herald' of the morn arises too,
> 'Post' after 'Post' succeeds, and all day long
> 'Gazettes' and 'Ledgers' swarm, a motley throng.
> When evening comes she comes with all her train
> Of 'Ledgers,' 'Chronicles,' and 'Posts' again,
> Like bats appearing, when the sun goes down,
> From holes obscure and corners of the town."

The most successful of the new productions were *The Public Ledger*, started in 1760, to which Goldsmith contributed; *The Morning Chronicle*, commenced by William Woodfall in 1769; and *The Morning Post*, first published in 1772. "Memory" Woodfall had the gift of being able to compile a long account of a parliamentary debate without taking notes of the speeches. He would sit in the gallery with his eyes closed and his hands leaning on a stick, and then, without any interval, write a report of sixteen columns. When Woodfall retired from the *Chronicle*, in 1789, it was acquired by a young Scotsman of thirty-three, who had already been employed for twelve years in journalism, named James Perry.

Perry was the first of the great nineteenth century editors, "a man so genial and so accomplished," to quote Miss Mitford, "that even when

WILLIAM WOODFALL, OR 'MEMORY' WOODFALL, 1746-1803

Erskine, Romilly, Tierney, and Moore were present, he was the most charming talker at his own table"—a man, also, as Leigh Hunt remarked, who "not unwillingly turned his eyes upon the ladies." Under Perry *The Morning Chronicle* became for many years the most prosperous organ of the Whig opposition, numbering among its contributors Lamb, Hazlitt, Campbell and Coleridge. After Perry's death in 1821, and despite the ability of John Black, the paper declined, but it was revived by the Whigs in 1834 and did not disappear finally until 1862, having for much of its existence played an important part in affairs.

The Morning Post was started three years after the *Chronicle* and eventually outlived it by more than seventy years, but for a long time it made little headway against its rival. The *Post* was founded as a medium for commercial advertising by a syndicate which contained such familiar names as Tattersall and Christie, and for nearly fifteen years John Bell was one of its principal proprietors.

In Perry and Bell we have excellent examples of two contrasting types which have combined, throughout its history, to exert a profound influence on our journalism. Both were self-made men, but Perry's success was founded on his literary and social talents; Bell's on his skill as bookseller, publisher and printer. According to Leigh Hunt, Bell was "a plain man with a red face, and a nose exaggerated by intemperance," but he had a good-natured smile and an agreeable voice, and in his many enterprises showed excellent taste. He is equally to be remembered as a pioneer in type-design and in the art of popularising good literature; as the founder of *Bell's Weekly Messenger* and a fashionable illustrated magazine called *La Belle Assemblée*; and as the publisher of Bell's *Poets* and of similar editions of Shakespeare and *The British Theatre*.

Bell's connexion with *The Morning Post* ceased in 1786. Nothing creditable was to be expected of it under the editorship of the Rev. Henry Bate, the fighting parson, and his still less reputable successor the Rev. William Jackson; but when in 1795 Daniel Stuart, "frank, plain and English all over," bought the whole concern, plant, office and copyright, for £600, the great days of the paper began. With Coleridge and Lamb attached to the staff, and Southey and Wordsworth as contributors, Stuart was able to raise the circulation from 350 in 1795 to 4,500 in 1803.

In the meanwhile another and formidable competitor was finding his feet. On January 1, 1785, appeared the first number of *The Daily Universal Register*, which in 1788 changed its title to *The Times*.

JAMES PERRY

THE TIMES OR DAILY UNIVERSAL REGISTER
Detail from the heading of the 1st number, January 1st, 1788

VIII

When *The Daily Universal Register* came into being, there were already in existence eight other morning papers, founded between 1730 and 1780, and nine evening papers published three times a week. John Walter admitted in the first number that "To bring out a New Paper at the present day, when so many others are already established and confirmed in the public opinion, is certainly an arduous undertaking"; but he declared himself confident that he would find readers for a paper that was "the Register of the times and faithful recorder of every species of intelligence."

We have seen that the development of advertising and Wilkes's victory over the House of Commons had by this time brought the Press a measure of independence; but its emancipation was only in the early stages, newspaper readers were still largely coffee-house readers, corruption was rife, and the word 'journalist' still carried with it the worst associations of chicanery and political management. Under John Walter I, an enterprising but not entirely scrupulous business man, *The Times* behaved no better than many of its contemporaries. There is evidence that for ten years the paper received £300 a year from the Government, while as a sideline it did a little blackmailing and charged fees for the suppression of libels—a practice later brought to a fine art by such sheets as *The Age* and *The Satirist*.

It was not until 1803, when John Walter II was placed in sole charge of the paper, that *The Times* showed signs of responsibility. From the start John Walter II set his face against corruption; and gradually he released his paper from the tyranny of party subsidies and vested interests. Though an able writer, who for several years acted as his own editor, he was primarily a business man—one to whose honest example his successors in the London newspaper trade owe an incalculable debt. If he had a fault, it was that he was over-modest in his bearing.

While Walter was making his first moves towards full independence at Printing House Square, other reformers were also on the march.

Particularly to be noted were a group of young Liberals, schoolfellows at Christ's Hospital, who, under the leadership of Leigh Hunt and his brother John, gave their services to *The Examiner*, "a new Sunday paper upon Politics, Domestic Economy, and Theatricals, price 7½d.," which first appeared on January 3, 1808. Mr. Edmund Blunden has in more than one place sung the well-deserved praises of Leigh Hunt and his *Examiner*: here it will be sufficient to say that, from the first, it deserved to succeed—both for the dash and daring of its political articles and for the high standard of its literary and theatrical contributions. Of Hunt's personal qualities—

> "The Patriot's honest voice, the Poet's lays,
> The subtle Critic, Essayist refined,
> In all, brave, sympathetic, pungent, kind"—

William Allingham's lines are a reminder. In Fleet Street he deserves always to be remembered for the public-spirited, crusading zeal which his *Examiner* imparted, at the outset, to nineteenth century journalism.

These years also witnessed the development of the great literary reviews, publications which, though they may not come directly within the

THE TIMES PRINTING PRESS INVENTED AND CONSTRUCTED BY APPLEGATH AND COWPER, *THE TIMES* ENGINEERS, 1827

limits of our subject, cannot be considered apart from it. The Whig *Edinburgh Review*, founded in 1802 under the editorship of the delightful Sydney Smith, was followed in 1809 by the Tory *Quarterly Review* under the waspish William Gifford—*bête noire* of Hunt and Hazlitt—and in 1817 by *Blackwood's Magazine*. Among English publishers no name has a greater lustre than that of John Murray II, the founder of the *Quarterly*—a man with a dash of quick temper, who is said to have once hit his footman on the head with a leg of mutton, but of whom George Borrow declared that he wished "all the world were as gay as he." One moral of Murray's career, however, is that between the literary publisher and the newspaper-man lies a great gulf. When tempted into daily journalism in 1826 by Disraeli, Murray saw his *Representative* fail dismally.

We must return, however, to the group of former Blue Coat boys which centred in Hunt and Lamb, for it was from this group that arose perhaps the greatest journalist of the nineteenth century—Thomas Barnes. The son of an attorney, Barnes was born in 1785, probably in Southwark. After passing through Christ's Hospital and Cambridge, he studied for the Bar and contributed masterly critical essays, on the theatre, literature and politics, to his friend Leigh Hunt's *Examiner* and *Reflector*, and to John Scott's *The Champion*. Joining *The Times* in 1809, he became its editor in 1817.

It was a daring move on John Walter's part, at a moment when *The Times* was still in keen competition with *The Morning Chronicle*, to appoint an editor of liberal sympathies who could not be expected to conciliate his Tory readers. But he never regretted his choice. Barnes soon showed that he was not a party man, and that his guiding motives were patriotism, hatred of injustice, and a desire to serve the interests of the rising middle class. John Walter had fought successfully for the right to print the news without interference; Barnes's triumph in the complementary struggle for freedom of comment made him our first genuinely responsible and independent editor.

Virile, plain-spoken, scholarly, in some ways fastidious—often reminiscent of his own favourite Fielding—Thomas Barnes so far dominated the newspaper world that the course of English journalism in the early nineteenth century must largely be followed in the story of *The Times*. Although Lord Chancellor Lyndhurst described him in his life-time as "the most powerful man in the country," Barnes's supremacy can be better appreciated now than it could then, for it was not only upheld but at the same time obscured by the principle of strict anonymity in which he was so passionate a believer.

Barnes's task, it must be emphasised, had been greatly eased by the enterprise and efficiency of John Walter II. The paper already possessed a reputation for its foreign news, and the installation of steam printing machinery at the office in 1814 had placed *The Times* a long way ahead

JOHN WALTER II, 1776-1847
Miniature by an unknown artist

of its rivals on the mechanical side. To raise the reputation of the leading articles and the "letters to the Editor" were main concerns of Barnes. His collaboration with the Duke of Wellington to secure Catholic emancipation; his important share in the passage of the great Reform Bill; his friendship and quarrel with Brougham; the decisive support that he gave to Peel in 1834, and his aid in preparing the Tamworth Manifesto and launching the new Conservative party—all these belong to the history of the period as well as to the history of *The Times*. This lover of liberty and justice, whose Bohemian habits never compromised his high principles, not only gained recognition for the new profession of journalism but brought that "Awful Monosyllable" *The Times* to a height of power that it has never reached again.

Even during the long reign of J. T. Delane, who succeeded to the editorship on the death of Barnes in 1841, the prestige of *The Times* was never greater than in 1834.

All this was not done by mincing words:

"Newspaper writing is a thing *sui-generis* [said Barnes in a typical passage]: it is in literature what brandy is in the beverage: John Bull whose understanding is rather sluggish—I speak of the majority of readers—requires a strong stimulus. He swallows his beef and cannot digest it without a dram: he dozes composedly

LEIGH HUNT, 1784-1859
Engraving by A. Crowquill

over his prejudices which his conceit calls opinions and you must fire ten-pounders at his densely-compacted intellect before you can make it apprehend your meaning or care one farthing for your efforts."

As *The Times* advanced its position steadily under cover of Barnes's cannonade, the shackles on journalistic enterprise fell away one by one. In 1825 restrictions on the size of newspapers were removed; a page of *The Times* was enlarged to six columns, and eight-page issues alternated with the usual four-pagers: in 1833 the tax on advertisements was reduced, and in 1836 the stamp tax lowered to a penny.

Measured beside Thomas Barnes, prominent contemporaries in journalism are inclined to lose stature. William Cobbett, his most distinguished rival after the death of Perry, lacked the all-round ability to make a success of his evening paper, while his weekly *Political Register*, though it provided a sufficiently provocative leading article, could not compete with the news-gathering resources of *The Times*. In the words of Brougham's secretary, Denis Le Marchant, in 1834: "*The Times* was at this period without doubt the leading Journal in Europe . . . the other newspapers were comparatively insignificant."

We have no space to discuss journalists like Street and Merle of *The Courier*, who gave obsequious support to each party in power. But if two men were to be picked to represent the contrasting personalities at work in Fleet Street in the 1830's, we might choose that genial rascal Theodore Hook, facetious, scurrilous, but full of gusto, who in the best days of *John Bull* received as much as £2,000 a year; and the charming editor of *The Etonian*, Winthrop Mackworth Praed, a poet and politician whose polished leading articles in *The Morning Post* between 1832 and 1834 revived something of that paper's former distinction. They illustrate the depths and heights of journalism in these turbulent years, and the remarkable talent that was to be found at both levels.

GEORGE AUGUSTUS SALA, 1828-1896
Coloured cartoon by Ape from *Vanity Fair*, September, 1875

ALFRED HARMSWORTH, 1865-1922
Coloured cartoon by Spy, 1895
By courtesy of the London Press Club

IX

It says much for Barnes that by the end of his editorship a place on the staff of *The Times* should have proved acceptable to an ambitious, well-born young man like Roundell Palmer, later Lord Selborne. Barnes himself had stormed the citadel of the Athenaeum and had been entertained at a formal dinner by a Lord Chancellor. Respectability in journalism, though the chances of encountering it were still problematical, had at least been shown to be possible.

In 1841 John Thadeus Delane took charge of a thoroughly established journal, on a sound financial footing, with a circulation of about 28,000, far ahead of all rivals. He was the son of a barrister who for many years acted as financial manager of *The Times*. At Oxford he had been more prominent as a horseman than as a scholar, but his short apprenticeship at Printing House Square under Barnes must, as Sir Edward Cook says, "have revealed great readiness, judgment and resource." He was only twenty-three when he dashed into the room of his friend, John Blackwood, the publisher, and said "By Jove, John, what do you think has happened? I am editor of *The Times*."

We have said that the influence of *The Times* was never greater than it was in 1834 under the original "Thunderer," Barnes; but in the noisy years during which Barnes fought to win respect for journalism, his "ten-pounders" were of the sort that hit or miss. Under Delane the hard-won position was consolidated and the circulation expanded steadily. Delane introduced a quieter note suited to calmer times. By 1843 the paper had become "mild, argumentative and discriminating."

Delane was in many ways the antithesis of Barnes. While Barnes was himself a writer of unusual power, who chose his words like an artist, Delane wrote little in his paper. Barnes enjoyed the pleasures of his Bohemian life; Delane did not smoke and "drank wine sparingly." Barnes was the more fascinating, but also the more puzzling character; Delane was eminently straightforward—a man of robust commonsense and wide interests, a great worker who despite the claims of society remained devoted to his family. It is perhaps Delane's misfortune that he lived into the photographic era: the formal Victorian portrait reproduced in this book robs "Mr. Tonans" of some of his thunder and is an unexpected reminder of his passion for horses.

For nearly forty years, from 1841 to 1877, Delane devoted himself, even more completely than Barnes had done, to *The Times*. When Palmerston offered him a high place in the Civil Service, he commented to John Walter III "My whole life is bound up with the paper . . . I must either work for it or not at all." He has been described as the personification of the news sense; and by living at times in almost daily contact with two Prime Ministers, Aberdeen and Palmerston, he obtained such sensational

John Thadeus Delane, 1817-1879
Photograph by Ernest Edwards

coups as the exclusive news of the decision to repeal the Corn Laws. "No editor," as Mr. Wilson Harris truly remarks in his book, *The Daily Press*, "ever received confidences from Ministers of all parties over so long a span of years as Delane"—and their trust was never abused. The affairs of *The Times* office were so completely under Delane's control that it was not until he had been editor for twelve years that he even employed an assistant in the task of sorting and reading the editorial correspondence which occupied him for three hours each day. Throughout the eighteen-forties *The Times* so far outdistanced all competitors that in 1854 its circulation stood at 55,000, as compared with its nearest rival *The Morning Advertiser's* 6,600, and *The Morning Post's* 3,000.

This year, 1854, witnessed the virtual beginning of a fine tradition in British journalism—the tradition of the war correspondent. *The Times* and its great correspondent William Howard Russell are inseparably connected with the story of the Crimean War, in the successful issue of which they played such an important part. Russell met with the disapproval of the military authorities from the start, but at Scutari he pitched his tent alongside those of the British force, and though it was thrown down from time to time he always succeeded in getting it put up again close to the lines.

Sir William Howard Russell, 1820-1907
Cartoon by Ape from *Vanity Fair,* 1875

Already on April 8, 1854, he was writing to Delane that the management was "infamous" and that "the sick have not a bed to lie upon," and his articles developed into a complete exposure of our muddled conduct of the war. *The Times* supported Russell in its leading articles; Delane himself paid a visit to the Crimea; and the paper raised a fund for the sick and wounded which was placed at the disposal of Florence Nightingale. Russell's phrase about the "thin red streak topped with a line of steel" at Balaclava (not, be it noted, the "thin red line") has passed into the language. As the official history of *The Times* summarises it, the paper had been:

> "largely responsible for the Crimean campaign that had brought victory in the end; it had 'saved the remnant of an army'; it had destroyed one Ministry and forced important changes in another; and it had caused the removal of a Commander-in-Chief. Russell came home in a blaze of glory, to be 'lionized' as no journalist had ever been before."

It must be noted, however, that though Russell's messages in fact saved the country from disaster, they had also invited disaster by their outspokenness in matters of military detail. "Security" has long since intervened to limit the range of subsequent war correspondence.

In "Journalists' Corner" at St. Paul's, Sir William Howard Russell is named as the "first and greatest" of war correspondents, but journalists remember with equal pride Archibald Forbes riding to Pietermaritzburg with the news of Ulundi, Labouchère sending his messages out of Paris in 1871 by balloon post, or Mr. Winston Churchill's exploits in the South African War. With them must be numbered men like Melton Prior, Frederic Villiers, George Steevens (author of *With Kitchener to Khartoum*), H. W. Nevinson, and many more. The same honours are due to the men who have kept up the spirits of our troops in the field by giving them newspapers like the *Mafeking Mail* and the *Ladysmith Lyre*, or (in the war of 1939) the *Orkney Blast*, the *Tripoli Times*, and the *Eighth Army News*—whose edition announcing the capture of Tobruk General Montgomery himself helped to distribute to his men as they moved through Hellfire Pass in pursuit of the enemy.

We have already lamented the absence of any full account of journalism at the universities. But a book about British journalists in the front line, from Howard Russell and G. W. Steevens to A. B. Austin, who died near Naples in 1943, and Stuart Emeny, who was killed with General Wingate in 1944, is a still more urgent requirement.

X

The decade immediately following the death of Thomas Barnes saw the start of many new enterprises. On July 17, 1841, under the joint editorship of Mark Lemon, Henry Mayhew and Stirling Coyne, appeared the first number of *Punch.* Ebenezer Landells had the supervision of the drawings and engravings, and Birket Foster remembered him coming into their workshop "saying 'Well, boys, the title for the new work is to be *Punch.*' When he was gone, we said it was a very stupid one, little thinking what a great thing it was to become." G. F. Watts, the painter, travelling in an omnibus, saw a gentleman toss the first copy of *Punch* aside contemptuously and heard him declare "One of these ephemeral things they bring out; won't last a fortnight!" This suspicion of new productions is deeply engrained in us, and explains why so few copies of first issues survive. Of the first number of *The Times* under the title of *The Daily Universal Register* only one copy is known to exist—that in the Burney collection (now in the British Museum).

There is no room here to trace the absorbing history of *Punch*, with its memories of Jerrold, Tenniel, du Maurier, Burnand and Seaman. Nor can we consider the aftermath of the establishment of the great literary reviews—the spate of popular magazines that found conscientious readers throughout the nineteenth century, from the *New Monthly* and the *Metropolitan* to Dickens's *Household Words* and Thackeray's *Cornhill.* Likewise beyond

THE FIRE OF HAMBURG
Engraving from *The Illustrated London News*, 1st number, May, 1842

our scope is a century of illustrated journalism, from the *Illustrated London News*, founded by Herbert Ingram in May, 1842, to *Picture Post*. But it must be said that the *Illustrated London News* at once showed an enterprise that was to be typical of this branch of journalism. In 1842, as in 1943, a great fire at Hamburg made the news of the day, and, with the help of the British Museum, a reconstruction of the scene was prepared and published on the front page of the first issue.

The time was to come when news photographs would be wirelessed across the world in a matter of seconds. Already in the eighteen-forties important changes were taking place. The old express road coaches were being superseded for quick conveyance of news by the railways, and in its second edition of August 6, 1844, *The Times*—again a pioneer—thus recorded the birth of Queen Victoria's second son:

"THE TIMES-OFFICE, Tuesday morning
Half-past 8 o'clock

We have the happiness to announce that the Queen has been safely delivered of a PRINCE.

We are happy to state that Her Majesty is doing well.

We are indebted to the extraordinary power of the Electro-Magnetic Telegraph for the rapid communication of this important announcement."

For some time the telegraph was too expensive, and too limited in its range, to be generally employed by the newspapers. But this was a propitious era for newspaper development, and the supremacy of *The Times* began to be challenged. In 1846 *The Daily News* was launched, being edited by Charles Dickens for seventeen numbers, until he gave it up "tired to death and quite worn out." The abolition of the advertisement tax in 1853 and the final disappearance of the newspaper stamp in 1855, stimulated other competitors. A clear indication that the telegraphic system had become an integral part of journalism was provided by the appearance in June, 1855, a fortnight after the passing of the new Stamp Act, of *The Daily Telegraph and Courier*, price twopence, founded by Colonel Sleigh.

The early days of this paper were not propitious. Colonel Sleigh soon found himself heavily in debt to Joseph Moses Levy, his printer, who eventually agreed to take over the business in settlement of his claims. Levy removed the second part of the title, and by halving the price made the *Daily Telegraph* the first paper to sell for a penny. Leigh Hunt's son Thornton was an early recruit to the editorial staff—and though Thornton Hunt died in 1873, T. P. O'Connor was one who, as a young sub-editor on the *Telegraph*, remembered his "kindness and prudence." In the spring of 1857 there appeared at the office a vision in a chocolate-coloured frock coat, blucher boots, and "a black camlet vest, profusely embroidered with beads and bugles of jet"—George Augustus Sala, who was engaged by Levy to write occasional articles, and for the next thirty-five years provided a steady stream of essays, criticism and "leaders" for Peterborough Court. His "warning beacon of a nose" glows with new life in Mr. Ralph Straus's biography and in the Fleet Street gallery will make a pair to John Bell's. Nor must it go unrecorded here that Sala was one of the principal founders of the Savage Club and the first chairman of the London Press Club.

With the assistance of Sala, Edmund Yates, J. M. Le Sage, Edwin Arnold and others, *The Daily Telegraph* soon established itself. For its continuing prosperity it has owed much to J. M. Levy's eldest son, Edward Levy-Lawson, who in 1903 became the first Lord Burnham. The second Lord Burnham, who succeeded him in 1916, was as good a man of business as his father and his grandfather, and like them had a fine record of work for the journalistic profession. He parted with *The Daily Telegraph* to the Berry family in 1928.

In its first year of existence *The Daily Telegraph* showed a tendency (later overcome) to model itself on contemporary New York journalism, and a desire (later achieved) to cater for the "million." It invented the "box" system of advertising and charged an extremely low rate. Soon after the price of the paper had been dropped to a penny, it was able with truth to declare that its circulation among London morning newspapers was second only to that of *The Times*. Yet in the sixties and seventies the competition of the now forgotten *Standard* gave most alarm to the

T. P. O'CONNOR, 1848-1929
Cartoon by Spy from *Vanity Fair*, 1888

management at Printing House Square. An evening paper since 1821, *The Standard* had been converted into a well-edited Conservative morning journal, priced at a penny, and well calculated to appeal to the less prosperous of the readers of the threepenny *Times*.

It was becoming increasingly clear that *The Times* could not expect to hold its own indefinitely as regards circulation. The removal of the last hindrances to newspaper development—the paper tax of 1½d. per lb. went in 1861—showed results not only in the development of the *Telegraph* and the *Standard*, but in the founding of the *Pall Mall Gazette* under Frederick Greenwood in 1865, and in the improvement by Algernon Borthwick of *The Morning Post*, which set out with determination to capture the custom of the aristocracy.

The horizons of the country newspapers, too, were enormously expanded by the growth of the railway and telegraph systems. *Berrow's Worcester Journal* and *The Lincoln, Rutland, and Stamford Mercury*, founded at the close of the seventeenth century, were the pioneers among country newspapers. In the eighteenth century their numbers greatly increased. If we take the town of Glasgow as an example, we find that its pioneer newspaper,

The Glasgow Courant, of twelve pages, was first published in 1715 three times a week, at the price of 1½d. to the public and a penny to regular customers. From time to time over the next hundred years twelve other papers were published in Glasgow, and at one period as many as five were in existence together.

This is enough to show that even in the eighteenth century the influence of the local press was considerable. In the year of Waterloo the circulation of such papers totalled 375,000 copies. But no daily papers were published outside London until 1855, when *The Manchester Guardian*, a weekly since 1821, first began to appear each morning. The same year saw the birth of *The Liverpool Daily Post*; and in 1857 *The Birmingham Daily Post* was founded. *The Scotsman* and *The Glasgow Herald* were also converted into daily papers at this time.

Henceforth the provincial press, which has many levels and at its highest produces a national newspaper like the *Manchester Guardian*, must be distinguished from its forbear, the old country paper. But it would be unfortunate if there were no word of gratitude in this book for the English country newspaper—that fascinating, unaffected, refreshingly unpretentious repository of local information. Fleet Street may have no time for the scale of values which the local editor keeps behind the green-painted window of his office in High Street—nor, always for the old-fashioned virtues which go with them—but the local paper has contributed for centuries to the happiness and usefulness of the people.

CARICATURES OF THE LONDON PRESS

XI

We have noted some of the reasons why *The Times*, after holding a position of complete supremacy, eventually found itself *primus inter pares*. Barnes and Delane had made journalism respectable—but there were now plenty of new journals and new journalists. As the history of *The Times* remarks, it was the trade that had undergone a complete transformation, "Printing House Square had not altered." In the Franco-Prussian war the paper again had Russell at the front and was first with the news of the

J. L. GARVIN
Coloured cartoon by Sir Max Beerbohm, 1931
By courtesy of the Artist and the Proprietors of The Spectator

A FORECAST OF LONDON'S AIR RAID DEFENCE AS SHOWN AT THE WEMBLEY PARK EXHIBITION IN 1924

Coloured reproduction in *The Illustrated London News* from a drawing by Steven Spurrier

By courtesy of the Artist and The Illustrated London News

capitulation of Paris and the terms of peace—though there was a feeling that on the whole honours rested with *The Daily News*.

John Walter III had to take a great decision—whether to lower the price of *The Times* and enter the competition for the "largest circulation in the world" (soon justly claimed by *The Daily Telegraph*) or to retain the price and keep up the character of the paper. It was only to be expected of a man of his high principles, but it is to his lasting credit that he chose the second course, and would make no compromise. With its increasing number of pages, and its up-to-date machines, culminating in 1879 in the Kastenbein, *The Times* continued for many years to maintain its standard.

An important development in the last half of the nineteenth century was the growth of the news agencies, Reuters and the Press Association, which between them have come to account for a good deal of the matter published in the daily press. Reuters was a private enterprise founded by Paul Julius Reuter, a Jewish bank clerk, at Aachen in 1847, and soon afterwards transferred to London. The Press Association, formed by the provincial newspapers on a co-operative basis, came into being in 1870, when the Post Office took over the telegraph system. These and other agencies will never supersede a paper's own correspondents, but they have proved invaluable as a safeguard and a standby.

The newspaper world was being gradually but radically re-shaped. The *Pall Mall Gazette* foreshadowed a new popular press, and T. P. O'Connor's *Star*, founded in 1888, and *The Morning Leader* were clearer indications of its imminent approach. Comparable to this irrevocable change in journalism was the change in the famous view down Fleet Street to St. Paul's caused by the London, Chatham and Dover Railway's bridge across Ludgate Hill. There were those, like Samuel Butler, who found the effect "more imposing now than it was before the bridge was built.":

> "Vast as is the world below the bridge (said Butler) there is a vaster still on high, and when trains are passing, the steam from the engine will throw the dome of St. Paul's into the clouds, and make it seem as though there were a commingling of earth and some far-off mysterious palace in dreamland . . ."

Another modern bridge, another barrier across an ancient view, was the career of Alfred Harmsworth, Viscount Northcliffe. To it, also, Butler's romantic conception of a "vaster world" superimposed on the old may be the best approach.

Alfred Harmsworth was born in 1865, near Dublin, the eldest son of a barrister who left Ireland in 1867 and established himself at the English Bar. His father's health failing when the boy was fifteen, young Harmsworth and his mother—a remarkable woman to whom he was devoted—supervised the upbringing of a family of seven boys and three girls. Abandoning all thoughts of Cambridge, Alfred Harmsworth threw himself into freelance journalism, gained useful experience at a Coventry publishing house, formed a London publishing business of his own, and in 1888 founded a popular weekly called *Answers*, in which his brother Harold (later Lord Rothermere) joined him. Soon *Answers* was selling a million copies a week, and making £50,000 a year and the financial foundations of the Amalgamated Press had been laid.

In 1894 the Harmsworths acquired and revived *The Evening News*, and in 1896, when the half-penny *Daily Mail* made its triumphant appearance, the new era in journalism was seen positively to have arrived. Harmsworth catered for the new class of inquisitive readers created by compulsory education, and he exerted himself particularly to interest women. Prizes were offered for gardens and homes; exploration was financed; motoring and flying were systematically and generously encouraged. Proper attention was at last paid to type and arrangement of a page.

By 1900 the circulation of *The Daily Mail* was approaching the million. G. W. Steevens gained many readers for the paper during the South African war. An edition was published in Manchester and the *Continental Daily Mail* was established in Paris. In 1903 *The Daily Mirror* appeared. Soon Lord Northcliffe (for such Harmsworth became in 1905) entered the newsprint business in Newfoundland on the largest scale.

XII

The success of *The Daily Mail* brought imitators and rivals. In 1900 Arthur Pearson founded *The Daily Express* (acquired by Lord Beaverbrook in 1915), and in 1904 *The Daily News* and *The Daily Chronicle* both joined the ranks of half-penny papers. Meanwhile *The Times* had fallen into serious difficulties. Isolated *coups*, such as that of de Blowitz in obtaining the text of the Treaty of Berlin, had been more than offset by the disaster in 1887 of the publication of the forged letter attributed to Parnell. It was not so much that the leadership of the paper was at fault under Thomas Chenery and G. E. Buckle, but that unbusinesslike methods, loss of advertisement revenue, and the enormous costs of the Parnell Commission had so far reduced its financial position that even the most capable and ingenious of managers, C. F. Moberly Bell, was hard put to it to make the books balance. In 1907, by which time the circulation had been lowered to 40,000, the Court of Chancery ordered a sale. Various attempts were made to gain control of the paper, and secrecy enveloped the negotiations, but early in the following year mysterious motor-cars might have been seen to stop near lanes in Hampstead, where two men would get out and walk up and down talking like conspirators.

The two men were Moberly Bell and Lord Northcliffe—and it was not long before Northcliffe paid £320,000 into the Bank of England in the name of Moberly Bell, and after one hundred and twenty-three years the

LORD BEAVERBROOK
Cartoon by David Low

controlling interest in *The Times* passed out of the hands of the Walter family. Almost overnight the magic worked: Monotype machines and huge Goss presses arrived at Printing House Square; no effort was spared to make the paper attractive. Having a declared admiration for Thomas Barnes and a deep respect for the traditions of *The Times*, Lord Northcliffe's main concern was with the methods of presenting the news. He never ceased to stress the importance of "topicality." There are still those who maintain that "Northcliffe ruined *The Times*," but this verdict, as Geoffrey Dawson emphasises in the Dictionary of National Biography, is "manifestly grotesque. The truth is that at a critical moment he was wholly responsible for saving it from extinction; but it is also true that his association with it had lasted long enough when he died and that another change of proprietorship was needed to add steadiness to vitality."

On Lord Northcliffe's death in 1922 the controlling interest in the paper was acquired by Colonel J. J. Astor, with whom Mr. John Walter, the great-great-grandson of the founder, was associated. By a trust agreement a committee of five—including the Lord Chief Justice, the Warden of All Soul's College, Oxford, and the Governor of the Bank of England—was formed to ensure that in the event of any further transfer of the controlling shares, *The Times* should fall into no unworthy hands, and that its independence should be preserved. Since 1922 its editorial integrity has been entirely above suspicion. Small in circulation, it has been great in influence.

C. P. SCOTT, 1846-1931
Bronze by Jacob Epstein

XIII

It is an invidious task to select for special mention a few from the many distinguished journalists of the last fifty years, but, by any standards of comparison, certain individuals stand out from the rest. Among them are three who fall naturally into a group:—W. T. Stead, editor of the *Pall Mall Gazette* and founder of the *Review of Reviews*, who was drowned in the *Titanic*; Sir Edward Cook, biographer of Delane, who succeeded Stead on the *Pall Mall* and then edited the *Westminster Gazette* and the *Daily News*; and J. A. Spender, who succeeded Cook on the *Westminster Gazette* and edited it for twenty-six years. With Spender may well be mentioned Sir F. C. Gould and Charles Geake, his coadjutors on a paper which will always be remembered with respect.

Great names are those of H. W. Massingham, successively editor of the *Star*, the *Daily Chronicle*, and the *Nation*, and Mr. A. G. Gardiner, who edited *The Daily News* from 1902 to 1919. For more than thirty years Mr. J. L. Garvin edited *The Observer*—a paper which, like *The Sunday Times* (acquired by the Berry family in 1915), has been in existence since before the Reform Bill. For thirty years, again—1902 to 1932—Mr. R. D. Blumenfeld edited the *Daily Express*, and he watched it rise to the leadership of the popular press. Mr. H. A. Gwynne, "finest-tempered of editors," worthily upheld the traditions of *The Morning Post* from 1910 until 1937, when he had to bow before the financial storm and see his paper amalgamated with *The Daily Telegraph.* A brilliant journalist was Cecil Chesterton, who died in 1918; and much of the lives of those great men, his brother G. K. Chesterton and Mr. Hilaire Belloc have been given to vigorous journalism.

Geoffrey Dawson, Mr. H. Wickham Steed, and Mr. R. M. Barrington-Ward, as editors of *The Times*, are *ipso facto* a part of the journalistic history of these years. But by common consent there is one name that o'ertops all others—the name of Charles Prestwich Scott, of *The Manchester Guardian*, who in the course of fifty-seven years as editor raised his paper from a place of purely local influence to one of national, and indeed international importance. This invincible and truly noble man, who at the age of seventy-eight was still to be seen bicycling home after a long night's work, once laid down in a speech these ideals for journalism and its practitioners:

> "Fundamentally it implies honesty, cleanness, courage, fairness, and a sense of duty to the reader and the community. The newspaper is of necessity something of a monopoly, and its first duty is to shun the temptations of a monopoly. Its primary office is the gathering of news. At the peril of its soul it must see that the supply is not tainted. Neither in what it gives, nor in what it does not give, nor in the mode of presentation, must the unclouded face of truth suffer wrong. Comment is free, but facts are sacred. Propaganda, so called, by this means is hateful. The voice of opponents, no less than that of friends, has a right to be heard. Comment is also justly subject to a self-imposed restraint. It is well to be frank; it is even better to be fair."

C. P. Scott and his successor W. P. Crozier fully lived up to these high ideals. On the whole they are approved and conformed to by our modern newspaper press. Yet the rise in this century of the great newspaper groups has certainly threatened the principles of editorial responsibility and of a newspaper's consistency of outlook, which were established with such difficulty by men like the Walters, Barnes, Delane and Scott.

Since the year 1900 the ownership of the press has been steadily consolidated. Three Liberal papers, the *Westminster*, the *News*, and the *Chronicle*, are now represented by one—the *News-Chronicle*. The *Telegraph* and the *Post* have been amalgamated. Three only of the eight London evening newspapers in existence in 1900 have survived. The old *Standard*, once such a thorn in the flesh of Delane and Mowbray Morris at Printing House Square, has been absorbed into the *Evening Standard*. Of the eight London daily papers published in 1900, only *The Times*, *Daily Mail*, and *Daily Express* now maintain their separate existence.

Distinct tributaries to the main stream of journalism in the British Isles are the ninety-two evening and the twelve Sunday papers. Of the latter, *The Sunday Times* and *The Observer* are the first in quality, and, as we have seen, they boast the longest histories. But the *News of the World* and the *People* have by far the largest circulations, each selling more than three million copies a week. The success of the Sunday newspapers may be due, in part, to their combining the attractions of a weekly periodical and of a daily paper—without the additional sense of responsibility which daily publication induces.

Until 1937 it was correct to describe the main newspaper combines as the Harmsworth, Berry, Odhams, Cadbury and Beaverbrook groups; but in that year the Berry group divided its interests between Lord Camrose (who controls the *Daily Telegraph* and the *Financial Times*), Lord Kemsley (controlling the *Daily Sketch* and *Sunday Times*) and Lord Iliffe, who has been mainly concerned with directories and trade publications, but who in 1943 purchased *The Birmingham Post*. This splitting-up of interests, as well as the breaking of the association between the *Daily Mail* and the *Daily Mirror*, has been welcomed by many as a sign that consolidation has reached its limit and is now in reverse.

At the head of Odham's Press, which has a controlling interest in the *Daily Herald*, stands Lord Southwood. The Cadbury family are in control of Daily News, Limited, which owns the *News-Chronicle* and the *Star*. Lord Beaverbrook's group, consisting of *The Daily Express*, *The Sunday Express*, and *The Evening Standard*, is more strictly individual than the others. In his book "Politicians and the Press" Lord Beaverbrook claims to have first become " a full-blooded journalist" after his retirement from the Government in 1918, but he had acquired the controlling shares of the *Express* for £17,500 some years before, on the advice of Lord Rothermere, whom he consulted on "a black Saturday's winter evening." The circulation was then 350,000 copies; by 1944 it had risen to 3,000,000.

Some of these proprietors style themselves "Editors-in-Chief" of the newspapers they own; beneath them are the nominal "Editors." The danger to genuine editorial independence and responsibility arising from these circumstances is obvious. The risk that a newspaper may be treated simply as a piece of commercial property has been removed in the case of *The Times*, as we have seen, by the formation of a legal trust imposing safeguards as to future ownership, and this idea has also been adopted by *The Observer*, *The Spectator* and *The Economist*.

LUDGATE BRIDGE AND ST. PAUL'S AS SEEN FROM FLEET STREET
Etching by Dorothy Sweet

XIV

When all is said and done, the future of journalism calls for no despondency. The personal integrity of British journalists—organised now into the Institute of Journalists and the National Union of Journalists—is further from reproach than at any time in their chequered history. Journalists may well be proud of the way Fleet Street stood up to the General Strike of 1926 (*The Times* did not miss an issue, though it relied on secretly installed multigraph machines for one number) and to the air raids of 1940-41 (which did not prevent the publication of any London daily paper for a single day). Gordon Robbins's *Fleet Street Blitzkrieg Diary* gives some indication of the extent of that emergency.

Greatly to the credit of the whole journalistic profession, indeed, is the way in which it has adapted itself to the extraordinary difficulties of this latest war—whether by buying its own ships to bring newsprint from Canada, by co-operating faithfully with the Censor, or by making resourceful use of much reduced space. Considerable, even sensational developments in newspaper production may be expected in the post-war years—as the enterprise of *The Times* in publishing a thin-paper air edition in 1944 indicates; but there are many who hope that, as regards the number of their pages, the newspapers will make a wise compromise between the leanness of war-time and the prolixity of peace.

The British public, for its part, has been loyal to the Press, and it may be conjectured that it will remain loyal. The newspaper habit is deeply engrained. How well C. S. Calverley understood us when he wrote of the weary clerk sitting happily on the seashore, on his first holiday for forty years, who:

> "laugh'd again, and softly drew
> That Morning Herald that he'd bought
> Forth from his breast, and read it through."

The development of wireless has caused the newspapers less trouble than some people had expected. It is true that at the very moment that the newspaper boy pushes the morning paper through the letter-box in countless English streets, the voice of a B.B.C. announcer may be heard, on the other side of the curtains, giving a piece of news much later than anything the paper contains. (What would Nathaniel Butter have thought of this astonishing challenge—or Thomas Barnes?) Yet the paper is not despised on this account. On the contrary, it is pulled through the slit with enthusiasm and scanned with avidity.

Even our enemies have seen fit to praise our journalism. "The English Press in its totality may be described as sound," wrote a German, Kurt von Stutterheim, in 1934. And an Italian, J. Sebezio, writing in 1937, though he deprecated the British treatment of "foreign politicians who are not bound to the British chariot," praised "the sobriety with which domestic subjects however grave are discussed, the indulgence with which are treated men of whatever party who make mistakes . . ."

In the course of three hundred years, British journalists from Muddiman and Defoe to Delane and C. P. Scott have learned to perfect their calling. May its grave responsibilities, as well as its great traditions, inspire the journalists of the future to go forward as bravely as some we have named. Freedom of the Press has not been won to be given away. To those who would venture to teach them their business, or would subordinate it to an upstart science called "public relations," journalists might well reply with a memorable paraphrase from Kai Lung: "Refrain from instructing your venerated ancestress in the art of extracting nutrition from a coconut."

A SHORT BIBLIOGRAPHY

J. B. Williams : *History of English Journalism to the Foundation of the Gazette*

J. G. Muddiman : *The King's Journalist*, 1659-1689 (Henry Muddiman)

H. R. Fox Bourne : *English Newspapers*

S. Morison : *The English Newspaper*, 1622-1932 ; *Ichabod Dawks and his News-Letter* 1635-1731; *John Bell*, 1745-1831

Anon : *History of The Times ; The Thunderer in the Making*, 1785-1841 ; *The Tradition Established*, 1841-1884

W.H.Hindle: *The Morning Post*, 1772-1937

Sir Edward Cook : *Delane of The Times*

R. Straus : *Sala: Portrait of an Eminent Victorian*

J. B. Atkins : *Life of Sir William Howard Russell*

J. L. Hammond : *C. P. Scott of The Manchester Guardian*

H. Wilson Harris : *The Daily Press*

P.E.P. Report on the British Press